Natures Three Daughters by Margaret Cavendish

Beauty, Love & Wit

Part I (of II)

Margaret Lucas Cavendish, Duchess of Newcastle-upon-Tyne was born in 1623 in Colchester, Essex into a family of comfortable means.

As the youngest of eight children she spent much time with her siblings. Margaret had no formal education but she did have access to scholarly libraries and tutors, although she later said the children paid little attention to the tutors, who were there 'rather for formality than benefit'.

From an early age Margaret was already assembling her thoughts for future works despite the then conditions of society that women did not partake in public authorship. For England it was also a time of Civil War. The Royalists were being pushed back and Parliamentary forces were in the ascendancy.

Despite these obvious dangers, when Queen Henrietta Maria was in Oxford, Margaret asked her mother for permission to become one of her Ladies-in-waiting. She was accepted and, in 1644, accompanied the Queen into exile in France. This took her away from her family for the first time.

Despite living at the Court of the young King Louis XIV, life for the young Margaret was not what she expected. She was far from her home and her confidence had been replaced by shyness and difficulties fitting in to the grandeur of her surroundings and the eminence of her company.

Margaret told her mother she wanted to leave the Court. Her mother was adamant that she should stay and not disgrace herself by leaving. She provided additional funds for her to make life easier. Margaret remained. It was now also that she met and married William Cavendish who, at the time, was the Marquis of Newcastle (and later Duke). He was also 30 years her senior and previously married with two children.

As Royalists, a return to life in England was not yet possible. They would remain in exile in Paris, Rotterdam and Antwerp until the restoration of the crown in 1660 although Margaret was able to return for attention to some estate matters.

Along with her husband's brother, Sir Charles Cavendish, she travelled to England after having been told that her husband's estate (taken from him due to his being a royalist) was to be sold and that she, as his wife, would receive some benefit of the sale. She received nothing. She left England to be with her husband again.

The couple were devoted to each other. Margaret wrote that he was the only man she was ever in love with, loving him not for title, wealth or power, but for merit, justice, gratitude, duty, and fidelity. She also relied upon him for support in her career. The marriage provided no children despite efforts made by her physician to overcome her inability to conceive.

Margaret's first book, 'Poems and Fancies', was published in 1653; it was a collection of poems, epistles and prose pieces which explores her philosophical, scientific and aesthetic ideas.

For a woman at this time writing and publishing were avenues they had great difficulty in pursuing. Added to this was Margaret's range of subjects. She wrote across a number of issues including gender, power, manners, scientific method, and philosophy.

She always claimed she had too much time on her hands and was therefore able to indulge her love of writing. As a playwright she produced many works although most are as closet dramas. (This is a play not intended to be performed onstage, but instead read by a solitary reader or perhaps out loud in a small group. For Margaret the rigours of exile, her gender and Cromwell's closing of the theatres mean this was her early vehicle of choice and, despite these handicaps, she became one of the most well-known playwrights in England)

Her utopian romance, 'The Blazing World', (1666) is one of the earliest examples of science fiction. Margaret also published extensively in natural philosophy and early modern science; at least a dozen books.

She was the first woman to attend a meeting at Royal Society of London in 1667 and she criticized and engaged with members and philosophers Thomas Hobbes, René Descartes, and Robert Boyle.

Margaret was always defended against any criticism by her husband and he also contributed to some of her works. She also gives him credit as her writing tutor.

Perhaps a little strangely she said her ambition despite her shyness, was to have everlasting fame. During her career, from the mid 1650's until her death, she was prolific. In recent decades her work has undergone a resurgence of interest propelled mainly by her ground-breaking attitude and accomplishments in those male straitened times.

Margaret Cavendish died on 15th December 1673 and was buried at Westminster Abbey.

Index of Contents

NATURES THREE DAUGHTERS, BEAUTY, LOVE & WIT

PART I

THE ACTORS NAMES
Monsieur Nobilissimo
Monsieur Esperance
Monsieur Phantasie
Monsieur Poverty
Monsieur Adviser, and several other Gentlemen.
Admiration - Madamoiselle La Belles Wooer.
Vainglory - Madamoiselle La Belles Wooer
Pride - Madamoiselle La Belles Wooer
Ambition - Madamoiselle La Belles Wooer
Madamoiselle Esperance, Wife to Monsieur Esperance
Madamoiselle La Belle
Madamoiselle Amour
Madamoiselle Grand Esprit
Madamoiselle Bon
Madamoiselle Tell-truth
Madamoiselle Spightfull
Madamoiselle Detractor
Madamoiselle Malicious

ACT I

SCENE I

Enter **MADAMOISELLE DETRACTIOR, MADAMOISELLE SPIGHTFULL, MADAMOISELLE MALICIOUS**, and **MADAMOISELLE TELL-TRUTH**

MADAMOISELLE TELL-TRUTH

The Lady Natures Daughters are the only Ladies that are admired, praised, adored, worshiped, and sued to; all other women are despised.

MADAMOISELLE SPIGHTFULL
We may go into a Nunnery; for we shall never get Servants, nor Husbands, as long as they live.

MADAMOISELLE TELL-TRUTH
Why there are but three of them, and three women cannot serve and content all the men in the World.

MADAMOISELLE DETRACTIOR
No, but they may discontent all the men so much, as to make them all to be Male-contented Lovers, who will reject all, because they cannot have what they desire.

MADAMOISELLE MALICIOUS
Let us make a Faction against them.

MADAMOISELLE SPIGHTFULL
Alas what Faction against them, can hurt and destroy Love, Wit, and Beauty?

MADAMOISELLE DETRACTIOR
Jealousy will weaken Love, Dispraise will disgrace Wit, and Beauty, Time will soon bring that to decay.

MADAMOISELLE TELL-TRUTH
But Jealousy cannot weaken true and virtuous Love, nor Dispraise cannot disgrace pure Wit, nor Time cannot decay the Beauty of the mind; wherefore all the faction you can make against them, will do them no hurt; besides, you will be condemned by all the Masculine Sex, if not punished with infamy, for your treachery; and since you cannot do them harm, your best way will be to imitate them for your own good.

MADAMOISELLE SPIGHTFULL
So we shall be laughed at, and stared on as Monkies, and scorned; forasmuch as we offer at that which is beyond our abilities, and whatsoever is forced, and constrained, appeareth ridiculous.

MADAMOISELLE MALICIOUS
Come let us leave speaking of them, and thinking of them, if we can.

[Exeunt.

SCENE II

Enter **MONSIEUR ESPERANCE**, and his Wife **MADAMOISELLE ESPERANCE**.

MONSIEUR ESPERANCE
Surely Wife you do not love me, you are not any way kind to me.

MADAMOISELLE ESPERANCE

True Love Husband, is not so fond as serviceable.

MONSIEUR ESPERANCE
But true Love will express it self sometimes: for if you did truly Love me, you would hang about my Neck, as if you meant to dwell there.

MADAMOISELLE ESPERANCE
If I thought my kindness might not Surfet your affection, I would hang about your Neck, as the Earth to the Center, and as you move should bear me still about you; but I am afraid if overfond, you should be weary of me, and account me a trouble, and I had rather starve all my delights, than make you loath my Company.

MONSIEUR ESPERANCE
This is but an excuse Wife.

MADAMOISELLE ESPERANCE
Why are you Jealouse, that you think my words speak not my thoughts? have I behaved my self so indicreetly, or have my actions been so light, as you believe I shall be wanton?

MONSIEUR ESPERANCE
No, I do not fear your Virtue.

MADAMOISELLE ESPERANCE
Do you fear my Indiscretion?

MONSIEUR ESPERANCE
I hope you will give me no cause to fear, although Husbands are oftner dishonoured by their Wives Indiscretions, than their Inconstant affections.

MADAMOISELLE ESPERANCE
Pray be confident, that I shall have a greater care of your Honour, than of my own Life.

[Exeunt.

SCENE III

Enter **TWO GENTLEMEN**.

FIRST GENTLEMAN
The Lady Natures three Daughters, namely Wit, Beauty, and Love, are the sweetest, and most Virtuous Ladies in the World.

SECOND GENTLEMAN
I have heard so much of their fame, as I have a great desire to see them.

FIRST GENTLEMAN

You may see the Lady Wit, for she doth discourse often in publick; but for the other two Sisters, they are somewhat more retired.

SECOND GENTLEMAN
How shall we know the time, that the Lady Wit discourses in publick?

FIRST GENTLEMAN
I am now going to see if I can get a place, where I may

SECOND GENTLEMAN
I will go with you, if you will give me leave.

FIRST GENTLEMAN
With all my Heart.

[Exeunt.

SCENE IV

Enter **MONSIEUR NOBILISSIMO**, and **MONSIEUR POVERTY**.

MONSIEUR POVERTY
My Noble Lord, I am a Gentleman, one that is ruin'd by Fortunes spight, and not by my own Carelesness, Vanity, Luxury, or Prodigality; for my Poverty is honest: but though my Poverty hath an honest face, yet it is ashamed to appear in the open light of publick knowledg, which makes me whisper my wants to your Lordships private Ear.

MONSIEUR NOBILISSIMO
Sir, if your necessities can conceal themselves, they shall never be divulged by me; and what I can honestly give you out of my Estate, and not very imprudently from my self, I shall freely, and secretly, distribute to you, and such as are in your condition.

MONSIEUR POVERTY
Your Lordships Servant.

[Exeunt.

SCENE V

Enter **MADAMOISELLE AMOR** alone.

MADAMOISELLE AMOR
The mind is the best Tutor, and ought to instruct the Senses how to choose; for the Senses are but as the working Labourers, to bring Lifes materials in; but O my Senses have betrayed my mind, in bringing

through my Ears, and Eyes, Beauty, and Wit, which like as creeping Serpents, got passage to my heart, and winding round about with flattering imbraces, yet sting the peace, and quiet of my mind, raising therein blisters of discontent, causing an anguish of restless thoughts, which work, and beat like pulsive pain.

But O had I been both Deaf and Blind, Then might I scape this Hell tormenting mind; His Wit like various Musick pierc'd my Ear, Some being solemn, and some pleasant were: And when he spake, his person did appear Like to the Sun, when no dark Clouds were neer; Fame of his valour, like a trumpet sound, Through Ears from Heart, unto the Eyes rebound; And then his person, like Mars did appear, Yet so, as when fair Venus Queen was neer. O Love forbear, use not this cruelty, Either bind him, or give me liberty.

[Enter **MONSIEUR ADRESSER**.

MONSIEUR ADRESSER
What are you all alone sweet Mistriss?

MADAMOISELLE AMOR
No Sir, I have the Company of thoughts.

MONSIEUR ADRESSER
Those are Melancholy Companions.

MADAMOISELLE AMOR
Indeed mine are so at this time; yet thoughts with thoughts may discourse wittily, and converse pleasantly together, without articulate words.

MONSIEUR ADRESSER
Certainly your thoughts must needs be pleasant, your words are so witty.

MADAMOISELLE AMOR
No truly, for my thoughts lie in my brain like a Chaos in a confused heap, and my brain being young, hath not enough natural heat to disgest them into a Methodical order; neither hath Time cookt them ready for the Mind to dish out, or the Tongue to carry to the Ears of the hearers.

MONSIEUR ADRESSER
The oftner I hear, and see you, the more I wonder at you.

MADAMOISELLE AMOR
Why, I hope Sir I am no Monster?

MONSIEUR ADRESSER
No, for you seem to me something divine.

MADAMOISELLE AMOR
Then you should rather admire me: for Admiration proceeds from things excellent, Wonder from things strange and unusuall.

MONSIEUR ADRESSER

So you are strange, and unusal: for things divine are not common; and certainly you are a thing illuminated beyond Natures Art, and are the only delight of Mankind.

MADAMOISELLE AMOR

Men take no worldly delight in Coelestial Creatures, but with Earthly; wherefore the most refined and illuminated, is oftenest rejected.

MONSIEUR ADRESSER

No Lady, they are not rejected, but as Angels, they will not reside with us.

MADAMOISELLE AMOR

Sir, for fear I should lose the Angelical opinion you have of me, I will depart soon as Angels do.

[Exeunt.

ACT II

SCENE VI

Enter **MADAMOISELLE DETRACTIOR, MADAMOISELLE SPIGHTFULL, MADAMOISELLE MALICIOUS,** and **MADAMOISELLE TELL-TRUTH**

MADAMOISELLE TELL-TRUTH
Come, will you go to hear the Lady Wit discourse?

MADAMOISELLE SPIGHTFULL
Not I.

MADAMOISELLE TELL-TRUTH
Will you go?

MADAMOISELLE DETRACTIOR
I will not go to hear a prating preaching woman.

MADAMOISELLE MALICIOUS
O that all the Masculine Sex would say as much.

MADAMOISELLE TELL-TRUTH
Let us go to learn Wit.

MADAMOISELLE SPIGHTFULL
I had rather be a Dunce all my Life.

MADAMOISELLE DETRACTIOR

So had I, if I must have none but a Woman instructor.

MADAMOISELLE MALICIOUS
Indeed women should learn, not teach.

MADAMOISELLE DETRACTIOR
It's a sign Men want wit, when they go to hear a woman preach.

MADAMOISELLE SPIGHTFULL
But let us go, if it be but to censure; for an hundred to one, but she will say something which may be contradicted.

MADAMOISELLE MALICIOUS
Then let us agree to be her contradictors: for whatsoever she faith we will confute.

MADAMOISELLE TELL-TRUTH
Nay by your favour, that you cannot do; for though you may contradict any argument, yet not confute it: for though Envy and Spight have bred Sophistry, yet Envy and Spight cannot confute the Truth.

MADAMOISELLE SPIGHTFULL
Well, let us go howsoever, if it be but to see, and be seen of those men as will be there to hear her.

OMNES
Content.

[Exeunt.

SCENE VII

Enter **MADAMOISELLE GRAND ESPRIT**, and her **AUDIENCE**. She takes her place, and then speaks.

MADAMOISELLE GRAND ESPRIT
Great Fortune, I at this time do implore, That thou wilt open every hearing door, Which are the Ears: let not my Wit be lost, For want of hearing, nor my words be crost, Nor yet obstructed by a busling noise, Or gazing, or observing some light toyes: But let their Ears be fixt, as if their sight Did view my words, till on their Ears they light.

Noble and Right Honourable,
I shall take my discourse at this time out of Ignorance, which discourse, I shall divide into Five Parts, the Gods, Fates, Nature, the World, and Man; for although Ignorance be obscure, and hard to be discovered, yet it is printed in a general Language, being spread and communicated over all the World. I begin with the First, and prime Creature, Ignorant Man. Man takes himself to be the most knowing Creature, for which he hath placed himself to the Gods; yet Man is ignorant: for what Man is, or ever was created, that knows what the Gods are, or how many there are? Or what power they have, or where they reside? What Man did ever know the Mansions of Glory, the Bowers of bliss, or the Fields of pleasure? What

Man ever knew whether the Gods were Eternal, or bred our of infinite, or rule, or govern, infinite Eternally?

Secondly the Fates. What Man is, or ever was, that knows the Fates? As whether they are Gods or Creatures, or whether the Fates are limited, or decree as they please? Or what Man is, or ever was, that knows the decrees of Fate, the links of Destiny, or the chance of Fortune, or the lots of Chance.

Thirdly. What Man is, or ever was, that knows what Nature is, or from whence her power proceeds? As whether from the Gods, or Eternity, or infinite, or from the Fates? Or whether the Gods, or Fates, proceed from her? Or what at first set her to work? Or whether her work is prescribed, or limited? Or of what she works on? Or what instruments she worketh with? Or to what end she works for? Or whether she shall desist from working, or shall work Eternally? Or whether she worked from all Eternity? Or whether her work had a beginning, or shall have an ending? What Man knows the beginning of Motion, or the Fountain of Knowledge, or the Spring of Life, or Gulph of Death? Or what Life is? Or what Death is? Or whether Life, Motion, and Death, had a beginning, or shall have an ending?

Fourthly the World. What Man is, or ever was, that knows how the World was made? Or for what it is made? Or by whom it was made? Or whether it had beginning, or shall have end?

The Fift and last is Man. What Man is, or ever was, that knows how he was formed, or of what composition, or what is that he calls a Rational Soul? Whether it is imbodyed, or not imbodyed? Whether it is Divine, or Mortal? Whether it proceeds from the Gods, or was created by Nature? Whether it shall live for ever, or shall have a period? Whether it shall live in Knowledge, or ly in Ignorance? Whether it be capable of pain, or pleasure? Whether it shall have a residing place, or no certain place assigned? Or if it have none, where it shall wander? Or if it have, where that residing place is.

As for the Body, who knows the perfect Sense of each Sense, or what mistake, or illusions, each Sense is apt to make, or give, or take? What Man knows how the Body dissolves, or to what it shall dissolve? What Man knows whether there be Sense in Death or not? What Man knows the motion of the thoughts, or whether the thoughts belong only to the Soul, or only to the Body, or partly to both, or of neither? What Man is there that knows the strength of passion? As what Faith may beget? Or what Doubts may dissolve? Or what Hopes may unite? Or what Fears may disorder? Or what Love can suffer? Or what Hate can act?

What Man is there that knows the Circumpherence of Admiration, the rigour of Adoration, the hight of Ambition, or the bottom of Covetousness? Or what Man knows the end of Sorrow, or beginning of Joy? And as for the Appetites, what Man knows the length and bredth of desire? As for the Senses, what Man is there, that knows the true Sense of Pleasure, or the uttermost bounds of Pain? Who can number the varieties of Tast, Sent, Touch, Sound, and Sight? What Man knows the perfect effects of each Sense? Or what Man is there that knows any thing, truly as it is? Yet certainly there cannot be an Athest; for though men may be so irrelligious, as to be of no Religion; yet their can be none so willfull, and utterly void of all Sense, and Reason, as not to believe there is a God; for though we have not the true light of knowledge, yet we have as it were a perpetual twilight; Man lives as at the poles of knowledge; for though we cannot say it is truly day, yet it is not night. Man may perceive an infinite power, by the perfect distinctions of all particular varieties, by the orderly production of several Creatures, and by the fit, and proper shapes of every several kind of Creatures; by their orderly Births, by the times and Seasons, to produce, flourish, and decay; by the distinct degrees, qualities, properties, places and motions of all things, and to, and in every thing, by the exact form of this World; by the prudent seperations, and situations of the Heavens and Earth; by the Circumferent lines and poyzing Centers; by their bounds and limits; by their orderly, and timely motions; by their assigned tracts, constant Journies, convenient distances; by their intermixing, and well tempering of the Elements; by the profitable Commerce, betwixt the Heavens and the Earth; by the different kinds, several sorts, various Natures, numerous numbers of Creatures; by their passions, humours, appetites; by their Sympathies, and Antipathies; by their warrs and parties; by the Harmony that is made out of discord, shews that there is onely one absolute power, and wise disposer, that cannot be opposed, having no Copartners, produces all things, being not produced by any thing, wherefore must be Eternall, and consequently infinite; this absolute, wise, and Eternal power Man calls God; but this absolute power, being infinite, he must of necessity be incomprehensible, and being incomprehensible, must of necessity be unknown, yet glimses of his power is, or may be seen; yet not so, but that Man is forced to set up Candels of Faith, to light them, or direct them to that they cannot perfectly know, and for want of the clear light of knowledge, Man calls all Creations of this mighty power Nature; his wife decrees, Man calls Fates; his pointed will, Man calls Destiny; his several Changes, Man calls Fortune; his Intermixing, Man calls Life; his seperating, Man calls Death; the Sympathetical, and Antipathetical motions of the Senses, and their Objects, Humours, and their Subjects, Man calls Pleasure, and Pain; the interchanging motions in Man, Men call Sense, and Knowledge; the seperating motions, Man calls Ignorance, Stupidity, and Insensibility; my application is, that this absolute Power, wise Disposer, and decreeing Creator, hath created himself Worship, in making Creatures to worship him; and it is probable, Truth decreed Judgment, Punishment, and Bliss, to such of his Creatures as shall omit, or submit thereunto: my exhortation to you is, to bough humbly, to pray constantly, to implore fervently, to love truly, to live awfully to the worship of this incomprehensible power, that you may injoy bliss and avoid torment.

[Exeunt.

ACT III

SCENE VIII

Enter **MONSIEUR NOBILISSIMO**, and **THREE** or **FOUR GENTLEMEN**

MONSIEUR NOBILISSIMO
I wonder who brought up that careless fashion, to go without their Swords; and I wonder more, how gallant valiant men, came to follow that fashion; for a Sword is a valiant mans trusty friend, to whose protection, he delivers his Honour, his Safety, and his Peace; for a Sword is a Mans Guardian, to maintain his Right, to revenge his Wrongs, or Disgraces, and his Mistriss, for whose service he wears his Life, and studies the worth and use thereof, and takes delight in the Honourable, and allowable practices therein.

FIRST GENTLEMAN
Faith my Lord I believe it was some Lover that brought up that fashion, who was loath to affright his Mistriss, with so dangerous a weapon.

SECOND GENTLEMAN
Some Carpet Knight upon my life my Lord.

MONSIEUR NOBILISSIMO
It was no true Lover; for certainly he would be sure to provide a safeguard, lest his Mistriss might be taken from him, or lest he should be affronted in her sight, which a Man of Honour, and a true Lover, will rather dy than part or suffer; and as for my part, I commend the Man that would neither eat, drink, nor sleep, without his Sword were by him, and made it his Bedfellow, and Bord Companion; as a friend that held to his side, and would fight in his quarrell.

SECOND GENTLEMAN
My Lord, if a man should do so in these times, his Neighbours would say it was out of fear, not courage.

MONSIEUR NOBILISSIMO
O no, for a Coward is affraid to use a Sword, and a Valiant man is affraid to be without the use, otherwise a strong sturdy Clown, might cuff him down, and kick him like a Football on the ground, which a Sword, and skill to use it, will prevent; for a Clown hath not skill to defend, or assault a Sword, having no practice therewith, nor ought they to have; for the use of this kind of Arms makes a Clown a Gentleman, and the want of skill makes a Gentleman a Clown; for a Right bred Gentleman, is to know the use of the Sword, and it is more manly to assault, than to defend; also to know how to mannage Horses, whereby we know how to assault our Enemy as well as to defend our selves; for it is not playing with a Fidle, and dancing a Measure, makes a Gentleman; for then Princes should dub Knighthood with a Fidle, and give the stick, and a pair of Pumps, instead of a Sword, and a pair of Spurs.

FIRST GENTLEMAN
My Lord, we are so far from wearing our Swords our selves now a dayes, as we give them our Footmen to carry, as if it were a disgrace to carry a Sword our selves.

MONSIEUR NOBILISSIMO
Tis true, and we are well beaten for our follies, for disarming our selves, and arming our Slaves; for now a Groom is made a Gentlemans equal, nay his Superiour sometimes; for if a Groom kills a Gentleman, the Gentleman dyes in disgrace, and the Groom lives with Honour, and gets the Fame of a gallant Person; for that is the phrase to all those that have fought, although they were forced thereto as Slaves, not distinguishing true valor, which is voluntary, temperate and just.

SECOND GENTLEMAN
Why then there should be a Decree, or Law, that none should wear Swords but Gentlemen, nor Arms allowed, but to those of approved merit.

MONSIEUR NOBILISSIMO
You say right, unless in time of Forein Wars, and then there should be a difference in their Arms; for if there be no difference of Arms, no difference of persons, and if there be no difference of persons, there will be no Supremacy of Power, if no Supremacy, no Royal Government; for as the Sword maintains the Prerogative of the Crown, so it doth the Honour of a Gentleman; and as the Sword keeps up the dignity of the Crown, so a Sword keeps up the Heraldry of a Gentleman; and no man ought to be accounted a Gentleman, that knows not how to use his Sword, and manage his Horse; for the one defends himself, and kills his Enemies; the other, doth front and charge his Enemy, and pursues him if need require.

[Exeunt.

Enter **MONSIEUR ESPERANCE, MADAMOISELLE ESPERANCE** and his Wife.

MONSIEUR ESPERANCE
Lord Wife you are very brave to day.

MADAMOISELLE ESPERANCE
I strive to be so every day.

MONSIEUR ESPERANCE
For whose sake?

MADAMOISELLE ESPERANCE
For yours.

MONSIEUR ESPERANCE
For mine? why sure that is not so, for certainly you would not take that pains, and bestow so much cost, for one you do enjoy allready, for a Husband that is tied to you for life, and cannot quit on Honourable terms; wherefore it is for one is loose and free, which you do strive by setting forth your self with garments rich, for to attract, and draw to your desires.

MADAMOISELLE ESPERANCE
The Circumference of my desires is only your delight.

MONSIEUR ESPERANCE
Why, my delight is in your Virtue, youth, and Beauty, not in your Cloathes.

MADAMOISELLE ESPERANCE
But Virtue is best acceptable, when Beauty doth present it; and Beauty finds most favour, when well attired; but were I sure you would like me better in mean Garments, and careless dresses, I then should Cloath my self in Freez, & like a Hermit my loose course Garments ty with single cord about my waste; but I will go and pull these Coaths off, since they are thought a crime, and I thought false for wearing them.

MONSIEUR ESPERANCE
No, I like them very well, if I were sure they were worn only for love to me.

MADAMOISELLE ESPERANCE
I never gave you cause to think I wear them for the love of any other.

[Exeunt.

SCENE X

Enter **MADAMOISELLE SPIGHTFULL, MADAMOISELLE DETRACTIOR, MADAMOISELLE MALICIOUS**, and **MADAMOISELLE TELL-TRUTH**.

MADAMOISELLE SPIGHTFULL
Madamoiselle La Belle is cryed up to be the only Beauty in the Kingdome.

MADAMOISELLE MALICIOUS
Lord that is nothing, for sometimes opinion will carry a black Blowse up to Fames high Tower.

MADAMOISELLE SPIGHTFULL
Yes faith, and most commonly they are cast down in disgrace.

MADAMOISELLE DETRACTIOR
Why should she be cryed up so? for she is neither well featured, nor well shaped, nor well fashioned, nor well drest, nor well bred, nor good natured; for she is of a brown Complexion, a heavy Eye, a sad Countenance, a lazy Garb; she dresses Phantastically, speaks Childishly, looks shamefastly; she is proud, reserved, coy, disdainfull, and self-conceited.

MADAMOISELLE TELL-TRUTH
Let me tell you, it is reported that she hath most lovely features, a clear Complexion, a modest Countenance, a bashfull Eye, a pleasing Speech, a winning behaviour, a Majesticall presence; besides it is reported that her disposition is civil, courteous, and obliging, her Nature sweet and gentle, her Education virtuous, her life temperate and Chast, her actions noble and wise, her discourse witty and delightful.

MADAMOISELLE SPIGHTFULL
Hey day, hey day, good Mistriss Tell-truth run not so fast in the wayes of vain Reports, lest your judgment fall into a Quagmire.

[Enter **MONSIEUR PHANTASIE**.

MADAMOISELLE MALICIOUS
Monsieur Phantasie, tis said you are one of Madamoiselle La Belles admirers.

MONSIEUR PHANTASIE
All the World would admire her, if they saw her, she is so Heavenly a Creature.

MADAMOISELLE SPIGHTFULL
If she be so Heavenly a Creature, she would be known to the whole World by the splendor of her Beams.

MONSIEUR PHANTASIE
Heaven is not made known to all; neither can the gloryes be suddenly comprehended, by weak Mortals.

MADAMOISELLE DETRACTIOR
Good Lord, if she hath such an infinite Beauty, that it cannot be comprehended, it is obscure.

MONSIEUR PHANTASIE

But those that comprehend least will be astonish'd, and struck with deep amaze.

MADAMOISELLE DETRACTIOR
I believe you are struck with Love, which makes you Blind, or Mad, that makes you think you see your own imaginations: wherefore fare you well, untill you are sober.

[The **LADIES** goe out.

[**MONSIEUR PHANTASIE** alone.

MONSIEUR PHANTASIE
I am struck indeed, for I am wonded deeper than Swords can pierce, or Bullets shoot at.

[Exit.

SCENE XI

Enter **MONSIEUR NOBILISSIMO**, and many **GENTLEMEN** with him.

FIRST GENTLEMAN
Your Lordship rid to day beyond Perseus on his Pegasus.

MONSIEUR NOBILISSIMO
No Monsieur, he went (if Poets speak truth) in higher Capreols than ever I shall make my Horse go.

SECOND GENTLEMAN
He might go higher my Lord, but never keep so just a time, and place, as to pitch from whence he riss, his feet in the same Circle, his leggs in the same lines, and your Lordship in the same Center.

MONSIEUR NOBILISSIMO
The truth is, my Horses went well to day; they were like Musical Instruments, fitly strung, and justly tun'd.

THIRD GENTLEMAN
And your Lordship, like a skilfull Musician, played rarely thereon.

MONSIEUR NOBILISSIMO
Come Gentlemen, let us to Dinner, for I have uncivilly tyred your Stomacks with a long fast.

[Exeunt.

ACT IV

SCENE XII

Enter **MONSIEUR PHANTASIE** as in a muse, sometimes Sighing, sometimes strikes his Brest, and sometimes turns up his Eyes; and at these postures Enters **MADAMOISELLE BON** at her approach he starts.

MADAMOISELLE BON
Sir, you may very well start to see me here, I do not use modesty, pardon me to be so bold to visit Men; it is the first visit I ever made your Sex, and hope it will be the last; but I am come, since neither Letter, nor Messenger, could have access to be resolved by your own Confession, whether you have forsaken me or not.

MONSIEUR PHANTASIE
No, I have not forsaken you.

MADAMOISELLE BON
But your affection prefers another before me.

MONSIEUR PHANTASIE
If I should say I did not, I should belly Truth, which baseness I abhor.

MADAMOISELLE BON
I am glad for your own sake you keep to so much Honour, though sorry, that you are no constanter, and more sorry for the Oaths you took, and Vows you made to me, since they became the witnesses of your perjury. I was not suddenly, nor easily brought to draw a Supreme Love to one; for before such time my Love was placed on you, my affections run equally in purling Brooks of Pitty, and Compassion, and clear fresh Rivulets of Charity and Humanity, from the pure Springs of good Nature and Religion; and hard it will be for me to turn this River to each stream again, if not, yet I shall be at rest; 'twill overflow my heart and drown me.

[The **LADY** goes out.

[**MONSIEUR PHANTASIE** alone.

MONSIEUR PHANTASIE
Oh I must curse my Fortune, and my Fate; lament my own condition to love without return, and only pitty what I loved most.

[Exit.

SCENE XIII

Enter **MADAMOISELLE GRAND ESPRIT**, and her **AUDIENCE**.

MADAMOISELLE GRAND ESPRIT
Great Mercury to thee I now address, Imploy thy favour, help me in distress; Thou God of Eloquence, so guide my tongue, Let all my words on even sense be strung, And let my Speech be tun'd to every Ear,

That every Ear each several word may hear: That every passion may in measure move, And let the figure of the Dance be Love.

Noble and Right Honourable,
I will discourse at this time of Love, not of the superfluous Branches, or wither'd leaves, or rotten fruits, but of the Root of Love, which is Self-love; It is the Root and Original Love in Nature; it is the Foundation of Nature, it is the Fountain from whence issues all the several Springs; Self-love was the cause of the Worlds Creation; for the Gods out of love to themselves, caused Creatures to be Created, to worship them: thus all Creatures being created out of self-love, and their chief being proceeding out of self-love, is the cause that every particular Creature loves themselves in the first place, and what Love is placed on any other, or to any other, from any particular, is derived from self-love; for we love the Gods but out of self-love, as believing the Gods love us; we adore the Gods but out of self-love, because we think we proceed from them, or were produced by their commands; we pray to the Gods but out of self-love, because we hope the Gods will help us in distress; we bless the Gods but out of self-love, because we do verrily believe the Gods will exalt, and Crown us with everlasting glory; and to shew that we Love the Gods, not as they are Gods, but for our own sakes, as believing they will or can do us good, is, that we are apt to murmure at the Gods, when we have not our own desires; we are apt to accuse the Gods, when any wordly thing crosses us; we are apt to curse the Gods at ill Accidents, Misfortunes, or Natural losses; we are apt to forget the Gods in the midst of pleasure; we are apt to think our selves Gods in the pride of prosperity; we strive to make our selves Gods in the hight of worldly power; and we do not only strive to make our selves equal with the Gods, but to raise our selves above the Gods, taking, or commanding to our selves more worship than we give unto the Gods; nay, those that are accounted the most holy and devout Servants of the Gods, belie the Gods, taking the name of the Gods to cover their own follies; as for example, whensoever any eminent person hath had ill success, either in, or after their Foolish, Ambitious, and Vain-glorious actions, they charge the Gods Decrees and pleasure, as it was the Gods will it should be so; like as she that Vaingloriously had her two and only Sons to draw her Chariot, like two Horses, or Dogs, or Slaves, and being both found Dead the next day, she had prayed to the Gods to reward them with that which was best for them, and being both dead, she said the Gods accounted Death as the best reward, when they no doubt dyed with over heating themselves, striving beyond their natural power and strength; yet these two Sonns that drew the vain Mother in a Chariot, drew and died out of self-love; either like as vain Sonns like their vain Mother, vaingloriously to get a fame, or believing the Gods would reward them for their Act, either with extraordinary prosperity, power, or blessedness, in the Life to come; and many the like examples may be given; for how ordinary is it in these our times, and in former times, for the politicks to perswade the people, with promises from the Gods, or to tell them it is the Gods commands they should do such and such acts, even such acts as are unnatural, wicked; and most horrid? thus Men bely the Gods to abuse their fellow Creatures. But most Noble and Right Honourable, my explanation of this discourse is, that since Self-love is the Fountain of and in Nature from whence issue out several Springs to every several Creature, wherein Mankind being her chiefest and Supreme work, is filled with the fullest Springs from that Fountain, which is the cause that Mankind is more industrious, cruel, and unsatiable, to and for his self ends, than any other Creature, he spares nothing that he hath power to destroy, if he fears any hurt, or hopes for any gain, or finds any pleasure, or can make any sport, or to imploy his idle time; he melts metalls, distills and dissolves plants, dissects animals, substracts and extracts Elements, he digs up the bowels of the Earth, cuts through the Ocean of the Sea, gathers the winds into Sails, fresh waters into Mills, and imprisons the thinner Ayre; he Hunts, he Fowls, he Fishes for sport, with Gunns, Nets, and Hooks; he cruelly causeth one Creature to destroy another, the whilst he looks on with delight; he kills not only for to live, but lives for to kill, and takes pleasure in torturing the life of other Creatures, in prolonging their pains, and lengthning their Deaths; and when Man makes friendship of Love, it is for his own sake, either in

humouring his passion, or feeding his humour, or to strengthen his party, or for Trust, or Counsel, or Company, or the like causes; if he dies for his friend, it is either for fame, or that he cannot live himself happy without his friend, his passion, and grief, making him restless; if Man loves his Children, Wife, or Parents, tis for his own sake; he loves his Parents, for the honour he receives by them, or for the life he received of them; if he loves his Wife, or the Wife the Husband, it is for their own sakes, as their own pleasure, as either for their Beauties, Wits, Humours, or other Graces, or for their Company, or Friendships, or because they think they love them; if they love their Children, it is for their own sakes, as to keep alive their memory, and to have their duty, and obedience, to bow and do homage to them; If Masters love their Servants, it is for their own sakes, because they are trusty, faithfull and industrious in their affairs, imployments, or for their own profit, or ease; and if Servants love their Masters, it is for their own sakes, as either for their power to protect them, or for the regard they have to them, or for the gain they get from them, or for their lives that are nourished, and maintained by them; if Amorous Lovers love, it is for their own sakes, as to please the Appetite, and to satisfy their desires, if Subjects love their Soveraigns, it is for their own sakes, as that they may have Law and Justice, Peace and Unity; If Sovereigns love their Subjects, it is for their own sakes, because they bear up his Throne with their Wealth and Industry, and fight to maintain, or get him power. My Application, most Noble and Right Honourable, is, that since we do all, and in every act for our own sakes, we should indeavour, and study, for that which is best for our selves, and the ground of our indeavour is to learn, and know our selves, every particular person must learn and know himself, not by comparative, as observing others, for every man is not alike; but by self study, reading our own Natures and Dispositions, marking our own Passions, mours, and Appetites, with the Pen of Thought, and Ink of Examination; and let the Truth be the Tutor to instruct you in the School of Reason, in which you may Commence Master of Art, and go out Doctor of Judgment, to practise Temperance; for Temperance keeps in its full strength, prolongs Beauty, quickens Wit, ripens Youth, refreshes Age, restores Decayes, keeps Health, maintains Life, and hinders Times ruines; but Temperance is not only a Doctor of Physick, a Physician to the Body, but a Doctor of Divinity, a Divine for the Soul; It preaches and teaches good Life, it instructs with the Doctrine of Tranquillity, and guides to the Heaven of Happiness; also Temperance is the Doctor of Musick, it tunes the Senses, composes the Thoughts, it notes the Passions, it measures the Appetites, and playes a Harmonious Mind. Thus Most Noble and Right Honourable, I have proved that Self-love is the Fountain of Nature, and the Original Springs of her Creatures, and that Temperance is the strongest Foundation of Self-love, although few build thereupon, but upon Intemperance, which is a hugh Bulk of Excess, the substance of Riot, wormeaten with Surfers, rotten with Pain, and sinks down to death with Sickness and Grief, not being able to bear and uphold Life; wherefore build your Lives upon Temperance, which is a strong and sure Foundation, which will never fail; but will uphold your Lives as long as Time and Nature permits them, and your Souls will dwell peaceably, and happily therein.

[Exeunt.

ACT V

SCENE XIV

Enter **MADAMOISELLE AMOR** alone as musing to her self alone, then speaks.

MADAMOISELLE AMOR

I will confess to him my Love, since my designs are Noble; but O for a woman to woo a man is against Nature, and seems too bold, nay impudent, only by a contrary custome; but why should not a woman confess she loves before she is wooed, when after a seeming coyness gives consent, as being won more by a Treaty than by Love, when her obscure thoughts know well her heart was his at first, bound as his prisoner, and only counterfeits a freedome; besides, it were unjust although an antient custome, if dissembling should be preferred before a Modern Truth, for length of Time and often practices makes not Falshood Truth, nor Wrong Right, nor Evill Good; then I will break down Customs Walls, and honest Truth shall lead me on. Love plead my Sute, and if I be deny'd, My heart will break, and Death my Face will hide.

[Exit.

SCENE XV

Enter **MONSIEUR ESPERANCE**, and his Wife **MADAMOISELLE ESPERANCE**.

MONSIEUR ESPERANCE
Wife, whither do you go? when I come near you, you always turn to go from me.

MADAMOISELLE ESPERANCE
I saw you not; for I had rather be fixt as a Statue, than move to your dislike.

MONSIEUR ESPERANCE
Why do you blush? surely you are guilty of some crime.

MADAMOISELLE ESPERANCE
'Tis said blushing comes unsent for, and departs without leave; and that it oftner visits Innocency than guilt.

[**MADAMOISELLE ESPERANCE** weeps.

MONSIEUR ESPERANCE
What do you weep?

MADAMOISELLE ESPERANCE
How can I otherwise choose, when my Innocent Life, and True Love is suspected, and all my pure affections are cast away like dross, and the best of all my actions condemn'd as Traytors, and my unspotted Chastity blemish'd with foul Jealousy, and defamed with slandering words?

MONSIEUR ESPERANCE
Prethy Wife do not weep, for every tear wounds me to Death, and know it is my extreme Love, which creates my fears; but you might have had a Husband with more faults.

MADAMOISELLE ESPERANCE
'Tis true, but not so many noble qualities as you have, which makes me weep, doubting you Love me not, you are so Jealous.

MONSIEUR ESPERANCE
By Heaven I love thee beyond my Soul, wherefore forbear to weep if thou canst stop thy tears.

MADAMOISELLE ESPERANCE
Tears may be stopt, unless they flow from an unrecoverable loss, which Heaven forbid mine should: yet sorrow oft doth stop the Spring from whence tears rise, or else the Eyes do weep themselves quite blind.

MONSIEUR ESPERANCE
Pray dry yours.

[Exeunt.

SCENE XVI

Enter **MADAMOISELLE BON** alone.

MADAMOISELLE BON
O Man! O Man! How various and Inconstant are you all, how cruell to betray our faint and unexperienced Sex, bribing our Judgments with flattering words, obscure our reasons with Clouds of Sighs, drawing us into belief with protestations, bind us with promises and vows, forcing us to yield up our affections; then murther us with scorn, and bury us in forgetfullness? but O how happy was I, before I was betrayed by Love? my heart was free, my thoughts were pleasant, and my humour gay; but now my mind is a Garrison of cares, my thoughts like runaways are wanderers. Grief on my heart his heavy taxes layes; Which through my Eyes, my heart those taxes payes.

[Exit.

SCENE XVII

Enter **MADAMOISELLE AMOR**, and at a distance seeth **MONSIEUR NOBILISSIMO**, she speaks first, as to herself.

MADAMOISELLE AMOR
Love and Discretion fight duels in my mind, one makes me Mute, the other doth perswade me to prefer my Sute; but why should I be nice to speak, or be ashamed to woo with words, when all our Sex doth woo with several dresses and smiles? each civil courtesy doth plead Loves Sute; then I will on, Love give me Courage, and Mercury guide my tongue.

[She goeth as towards the **MONSIEUR NOBILISSIMO**.

MADAMOISELLE AMOR

Noble Sir, impute it rather as a folly to my Sex and Youth, and not any impudence of Nature, if that my Innocency discovers my passion and affection, not having Craft, or subtilty to conceal them; but I must plainly tell you, no sooner did I see you, and hear you speak, but loved: but yet mistake me not, I dote not on your person, but your mind; for sure your Noble Soul shot fire through my Eyes into my Heart, there flames with pure affection; but for this confession, perchance you will set me as a mark of scorn, for all to shoot their scofs at, and in derision pointing, will laugh and say, there is the Maid that wooed a Man.

MONSIEUR NOBILISSIMO
Is this to me Lady?

MADAMOISELLE AMOR
It cannot be to any other, Nature could make but one, and that was you.

MONSIEUR NOBILISSIMO
If this be real you do profess, the Gods, should they have sent an Angel down to offer me their Heavenly Mansion, it had not been so great a gift as your affection.

MADAMOISELLE AMOR
Do you not hate me then?

MONSIEUR NOBILISSIMO
Nothing I Love so well.

MADAMOISELLE AMOR
And will you Love me ever?

MONSIEUR NOBILISSIMO
Yes ever; for when my Body is dissolved, Love shall live in my dust in spight of Death.

MADAMOISELLE AMOR
And will you love none but me?

MONSIEUR NOBILISSIMO
An intire and undivided affection, can be placed but upon one, and that is you.

MADAMOISELLE AMOR
May your constancy be as firm, as my Love pure.

[Exeunt.

SCENE XVIII

Enter **MADAMOISELLE LA BELLE** and her four Suters, **ADMIRATION, AMBITION, VAINGLORY** and **PRIDE**.

ADMIRATION

Dear Mistriss stay, that I may gaze upon you,
Then bow my knee, as to the rising Sun;
Heave up my hands, as when to Heaven I pray,
But being amaz'd, know not one word I say:
Yet superstitiously, I shall adore,
As my chief Goddess, shall thy love implore;
And being worship'd, you are deifi'd,
Your Godhead in your Beauty doth recide.

VAINGLORY

Thou absolute Beauty, for thy dear sake,
Of Lovers hearts, a foot-stool shall be made;
A Cushion soft, with Hopes fill'd full, then laid,
For thee to stand, and triumph on, fair Maid;
And Lovers Souls shall from their bodyes fly,
For thee a Couch, when weary on to ly.

PRIDE

Thy Lovers tears for to invite thy rest,
In murmuring streams, fall on thy marble brest;
And gentle sighs, like whispering winds shall blow,
And fan thy Cheeks, that Poets fire may glow:
Loves Melancholy thoughts, like Clouds of night,
Like as thy Curtains, drawn before thy sight;
For fear the Sun should trouble out of spight,
Thy Eyes repose, being the greater light.

AMBITION

Sweet Beauty, thou in glorious Throne shall set,
The spangled Heaven, seems but thy Counterfeit;
Thy Charriot shall be stuck with Eyes all gazing,
And oyld with Eloquent tongues, that runs with praysing:
Drawn by large strong well shapt Commendations,
Guided by Fame, about two several Nations.

MADAMOISELLE LA BELLE

Admiration, Vainglory, Pride, and Ambition,
Why do you woo Beauty, that is Deaf and Dumb,
That hears no praise, nor adoration;
It seeth no hands heav'd up, nor tears that fall,
It hath no tongue to answer Love withall;
It hath no Life, no Soul where passion lies,
It neither gives, nor takes instructions wise:
It is no solid Body you admire,
No substance, but a shadow you desire.

MARGARET CAVENDISH – A CONCISE BIBLIOGRAPHY

Philosophical Fancies (1653)
Poems and Fancies (1653)
Philosophical and Physical Opinions (1655)
Nature's Pictures drawn by Fancie's Pencil to the Life (1656)
The World's Olio (1655)
Playes, (1662) folio, containing twenty-one plays including
Loves Adventures
The Several Wits
Youths Glory, and Deaths Banquet
The Lady Contemplation
Wits Cabal
The Unnatural Tragedy
The Public Wooing
The Matrimonial Trouble
Nature's Three Daughters (Beauty, Love and Wit) Part I & Part II
The Religious
The Comical Hash
Bell in Campo
A Comedy of the Apocryphal Ladies
The Female Academy
Plays never before printed (1668), containing five plays.
The Sociable Companions, or the Female Wits
The Presence
The Bridals
The Convent of Pleasure
A Piece of a Play
Orations of Divers Sorts (1662)
Philosophical Letters, or Modest Reflections upon some Opinions in Natural Philosophy maintained by several learned authors of the age (1664)
CCXI Sociable Letters (1664)
Observations upon Experimental Philosophy & Description of a New World (1666)
The Blazing World (1666)
The Life of William Cavendish, Duke, Marquis, and Earl of Newcastle, Earl of Ogle, Viscount Mansfield, and Baron of Bolsover, of Ogle, Bothal, and Hepple, &c. (1667)
Grounds of Natural Philosophy (1668)